The HedgeHog

and

Other Selected Poems

by

Carl Scott Harker

The Hedgehog and Other Selected Poem

An Aldouspi Publication

Table of Contents

Introduction

Generally, I don't have a particular audience in mind when I write my poems. I write for whomever will read my work. But in reviewing the poetry I have published over the last few years, I noticed particular poems I thought I would have enjoyed reading when I was eight or ten or older. These are poems originally published to entertain or enlighten the adult reader, but I believe, now, they would also be accessible to younger minds.

There were enough such poems to put a book together and here it is: *The Hedgehog –* Poetry for children ten years and older. There are both silly poems and more serious poems here, and almost all of them, have accompanying illustrations added for this book. Although, the three poems featuring the photographs of Ansel Adams were inspired by their accompanying photos. And the title poem was also inspired by the included drawing of a hedgehog by Edward Lear.

Do you think that reading a poem is too challenging? Good poems provide clues to their meaning and incentives to read one line and then the next and then the next... And when you have reached the last line they provide a reward – which may be laughter, or wisdom, or a story, or a better understanding of yourself, and sometimes all of the above.

I think these are good poem in this book – and I think you will have fun reading them!

Art by Edward Lear

The Hedgehog

Happy is the hedgehog
As it goes about its day,
Rooting through the undergrowth
For bugs and slugs to slay.

Though cute, its fur is prickly,
And can be sharp when he's upset,
So learn to make him happy quickly
If you want him as a pet.

Despite the hog that ends his name
There is no pig within his soul
Though his snorting sound is much the same,
His nearest cousin is the mole.

So let the hedgehog wander wild and free
Or keep him as a pet,
In either case I urge you please,
To treat him with respect.

The Mermaid, Now Living on Land, Misses Her Ocean Meals

Come little shrimpies hear my call
And glide yourselves to me
Leave behind the dangerous briny, briny sea

In safety I will place you all
Into a case of steel and glass
(Once occupied by small mouth bass)

There in its water I'll throw your favorite foods
Like zooplankton, algae, worms and things decayed
You'll not go hungry on any day

Within the tank there'll be a tube
That shoots out bubbled air
To keep the water's oxygen levels fresh and fair

An aquarium attached bulb that's like the sun
Will bring you light and keep you warm
As you flick your tails to swim about alone or in a swarm

You'll amuse me and I'll amuse you
Will watch each other everyday
I'll sing while you dance, dance, dance in your shrimpy way

When time passes and you have grown
And the tank no longer has room for you to roam
Finally! I will crunch, crunch, crunch
And make my tummy your new home!

Poet Jokes

A poet was asked if he wrote free verse,
Of course, I write free verse, he replied
No one is buying my books!

When the poet heard about the company
Metaverse, he decided to invest in it.
Why? The poet never met a verse,
He didn't like.

Does a poet have to be poor, unloved,
Nearly homeless, smelly and work as a dishwasher
To write poetry?
No, but it helps.

Cat Claw Instinct

Patience,

I do my best
To love the dog,
Then claws
Scratch his nose,

Lightening.

The Little Girl with Dyslexia

Once there was a little girl starting school
She had dyslexia
She did not know she had dyslexia
Her parents did not know
Her teacher did not know
The school did not know
Doctors did not know
(Because no one knew to look for it).

And even though the little girl
Was very smart,
Having dyslexia meant
That the alphabet was a strange puzzle for her
Where "a's" were sometimes "c's"
And "s's" were sometimes "z's" and so on
And spelling, in general, was like entering a maze
Where words were always different.

Not knowing about dyslexia,
Her teacher taught the little girl
As you would someone
Who could distinguish letters easily –
Which was the wrong way to teach,
With the results being
Of a confused little girl

And a frustrated teacher,
"Why can't she learn, the way I am showing her?
"It's so simple," thought the teacher,

But the ABC's
Which can look like DHB's or AJZ's
To the little girl
Was not simple
(Nor would it be for anyone
Who had dyslexia).

So the teacher gave up and decided the little girl
Was not very bright and labeled her
"Retarded!"
Retarded is not a word we use today,
But long ago this word was used a lot.

For two months, the little girl was made to go
To a "Special School" for slow children
Where everything her
Special School teacher asked her to do
Was so easy, she could not understand
Why she was there,
Remember she was very smart.

Although all the other kids,
Except one boy who seemed smart like her,
Had trouble doing the lessons
And were well, slow,
The little girl tried to fit in,
But it was boring in class
And she was unhappy.

Luckily, one day,
A not very good teacher
Supervising the Special School's playground
At recess time,
Changed everything.

Here is what happened,
Because she could,

The teacher told the little girl
To sit down in the dirt,
But the little girl refused to obey,
She saw no reason why she had to sit down
During playtime,

Beside the little girl was wearing a new dress
And she knew that her mother would be mad,
If she got the dress dirty
So it could not be worn again the next day,
She could picture in her head
Her mother having to wash the dress
In the old washing tub
Which the little girl knew
Was hard work for her mother.
(It would be another year before her family
Got an actual washing machine
For remember, this was long ago.)

So the little girl would not sit in the dirt
And this made the teacher mad
And she grabbed the little girl
By one ear
And pulled her down,
And now comes the lucky part,
The principal of the school,
A black woman,
Saw what happened
And rescued the little girl
And after talking to the little girl
Soon realized the she was actually very bright,
And the very next day the little girl
Was back in the regular school.

Eventually, the little girl
Taught herself how to read and write
Though spelling continued to be a problem,
As she got older and had to write essays,
She would get "A's" for content and ideas,
But "F's" for spelling and grammar.

One year, she really worked hard on an assignment

Writing it over and over to correct any possible mistakes
And she ended up being accused of cheating!
Because it was so good,
Her teacher, a nun, could not believe
The little girl had written it herself.

But this unfairness did not deter
The little girl,

She adapted and survived,
And continued to get an education
Her dyslexia would not stop the little girl,

She developed special methods to compensate
For the way her brain worked,

Eventually, the little girl became a nurse,
Where she used hidden tricks
Like carrying a pen covered in white tape
With the alphabet written on it,
This was her secret tool to guide her
When she needed to file charts or other documents.

She took detailed notes when learning
A new piece of equipment or procedure,
Then used these written details to practice
Over and over
Until she could manage without the notes
Although she kept them in her purse,
She wore a bracelet on her left wrist
To remind which was her left and which was her right,
A useful distinction, when listening to the heart...

The funny thing about dyslexia
Is that it never wears off
Nor is there a cure
You can only compensate or manage it.

When computers came along,
What seems intuitive to you and me
Like "Cut and Paste"
Was not intuitive for her at all,

But a challenge,

Still she adapted
And learned to use the computer,

And the same was true for her smart phone.

Adapt and survive:

Each of us, I suspect,
Has an "invisible" challenge
In our lives
To which we must adapt
And then adapt again,
And this may make us look strange
Or odd at certain times to others,
And hence require a dollop of understanding
And tolerance
From everyone else.

Someday,
If love guides us,
The invisible differences
And the not so invisible differences
Between each of us all
Will become recognized
For what they are –
Treasured gifts.

PS. Here is a bit of dyslexic escapism...
One time, the little girl was asked to stand up
In class and recite the ABC's and she was trapped
And had to think quickly:
She started out with "A, B, C, D, Ng, Ymk, Rz, Kuo,"
When the teacher shouted, "What are you doing?"
"I'm saying it in Russian," the little girl replied.
The whole class, including the teacher,
Burst out laughing
And the little girl quickly sat back down
Before the laughter faded.

What Does A Spider Mean Within My Dream?

If you close your eyes and nod away
To a pleasant room
Where spider webs appear,
Just wave your arms about you
And brush them clear.

But if more webs around you grow
Alive with spiders running to and fro
And you see spiders black or green or gold
Scurrying on the walls
Or from the ceiling begin to fall
Or up your legs,
Eight-legged creatures crawl,
Oh, my!

And now the webs grow sticky and strong
And way too thick for your thin arms
To harm
And slowly enwrapped
You quiver and quake
The only escape
Is to become awake!

The meaning of this dream I'd say
Is a bug's revenge
And nothing more complex or deep,
I suggest what happened here, my dear,
Is you ate a spider in your sleep.

Cherry Tree Haiku

First tree blossoms bloom
Then pink petals like snow fall
Pies come in summer

In Billions of Years, There Will Be No Moon

The moon up there
Goes farther away
Each night,
According to astronomers
Through energy transfer
From the bulge of tides.

Silly Ocean Thought

I was on the beach
Gazing out towards
The horizon line
Of the ocean

It was early in the day
And the weather was
Still trying to decide
To stay chill or grow warm

When I noticed above the water
Way beyond the waves
A patch of fog pop up

It started a hesitant drift
Inland to the shore
Then dissipated

And it occurred to me,
Since it was that time of year
For whale migration,
That a pod of whales
Had farted
All at once

Which is just the kind
Of crazy thought
That an old man
Staring out at the ocean
Gets

Reading Makes a Difference

When I was young girl, we lived near a farm
And open land,
Where I traipsed and played with local kids
And visiting cousins,
But when the boys got too rough,
I liked to find a tree or large rock to lean against
And read the books I brought along.

Now, I write mysteries
About a government assassin
Who is a felinologist,
You would be surprised how many plot twists
A killing cat lover can have.

And for when the writing gets rough,
I bought a place to lean against,
My own organic farm
With open land, two kids, a loving hubby
And lots of cats,
Imagine that!

Free Will

What choices do birds make?
To fly with the wind or against it,
Which mate to pick out in the spring,
What lands to seek
To find food that is plentiful?

Hunger, shelter, reproduction
Drive birds, in much of their behavior,
But once the hatchlings have flown on
On their own
While the weather is still fair,
When a tummy is filled with worms
Or moths or spiders or seeds,

Does the bird on the branch
Or up on the rooftop
Have to chirp the song it sings
Or is that a choice of free will?

STICKY PORCUPINES

Roses are red,
Porcupines are sticky,
If you want to learn more,
Do a search on Wiki.

Forty-five Years Into the Void

How far is humanity's reach?
157.538189 AU and counting...
Where each Astronomical Unit (AU) is
≅ 93,000,000 miles.

One small construction
Of metal, materials and ingenuity
Is our species symbolic ambassador
Now traveled beyond
Even the reach of the Sun's
Electromagnetic influence
And slipped into the void
Of true interstellar space.

Tiny, brave probe out in the cold
Doing its job of relaying back home
Details of its ongoing current
environment
In scientific terms,
Speaking to us from
Almost 22 light-hours away.

And by its mission
And very existence
Saying, too, to any out there
Who can hear,

"We are here,
"We are here!"
The collective imagination
Of the minds of Earth
Made real
Called Voyager 1.

Voyager 1 in the Void (NASA Art)

The Samurai and the Three Ghosts

Inspired by this 1689 haiku:

Haiku by Matsuo Basho

On a journey ill,
My dreams wander far over
The withered cold moors

A light rain was falling and soon
The night would fall, too,
The samurai
Wounded and separated from the battle,
Which had moved east without him,
Wandered on a scant trail in the woods.

The samurai had poulticed and bandaged
His left side
Where a sword had pierced, in a downward thrust –
Less lucky was the attacker who lay dead
Somewhere behind,
But fatigue now hounded him,
A fever was rising,
And he hoped to find shelter
Where he could rest.

Then a clearing appeared
With a small hut of two rooms
Clean, but seemingly abandoned –
Much of the local population
Had fled the countryside
Due to the war raging around them.

Inside he lit a small fire to warm himself
And boil water for tea,
Which he drank while eating
Husked rice balls.

Near exhaustion, he explored the second room
To find the hut had further generosity to give,
He found a thin robe to wrap himself in –
Removing his still damp clothes
He put the robe on,
And there was a mat with a blanket –
He laid down,
His forehead burning up,
Sleep took him as the rain continued
To fall.

He awoke in darkness to something,
The drizzle of water had stopped,
He heard the sound of people,
Whispering lowly
Or as if far away,
His hands found his scabbard without thought
And released his katana,
He rose to meet the threat
Then stopped,
He recognized the voices!
Of which there were three.

One was his grandmother
Who had sung to him
Jovial songs when he was little,
Told him stories
And snuck him sweet snacks.

One was his mother
Who cared for his needs
And taught him patience
Hard work, honor and discipline.

The third voice was the melody of his wife
Who had brought him
Passionate love and cherished love –
The sweeteners of life.

But how could this be?
All three were dead
Sickened by one of the many plagues

That scourged the land in these times,
While he was away.

To make out what they were saying,
He moved closer, going into the front room,
There was scant light –
A slight redness from the last embers of the fire
Like a splash of red paint,
And a yellowish glow
Coming from the faces
Of his mother, grandmother and wife
Which was all he could see
Of what could only be their ghosts.

Each ghost spoke to him:
"We miss you."
"We miss you."
"We miss you."
And he was deluged in a flood
Of memories.

He remembered the words of childhood songs
And honey coated nuts and cinnamoned rice balls,
He remembered being taught to write
In the afternoons by his mother,
He remembered the embraces and kisses
And welcome homes of his wife.

He longed for the comfort of those days
The easiness of those hours,
He wanted to rest in dreams
Of happy times and laughter.

The ghosts said in chorus,
"Come with us."

And as they left the hut, he followed
The luminous faces of those he loved
Into the darkness of the night
Where clouds, though thinning,
Still shielded away
The light from the sky above.

"Hurry," they said as they moved
Towards the woods
And he was pulled along with them.

But a few more steps from the forest,
The overcast overhead finally broke
And a patch of sky opened in the clouds
And the rays of a full moon lit the earth
Where the ghosts and the samurai stood.

Horrified, the samurai watched the features
Of his most beloved ones
Transform into the heads of demons –
With distorted lips and cheekbones
Course hair and horns,
Blazing eyes and
Mouths filled with fang-like teeth,
Their jerking heads seemed to rest loosely,
On top of grotesque bodies
Made of green mist and slime
And shimmering spider webs,
Each pair of the demons' red eyes
Staring at him
Shot out burning rays of hunger and anger
That staggered the samurai.

It was the feel of the cold steel of his sword -
His forgotten katana,
Still in his hand,
That broke him into action.

The demons encircled him
And reached out to grab him,
Each slight touch of their hands
On his skin
Held the clammy iciness of death.

The samurai backed and ducked and swirled
And swung the biting edge of the katana
Only to have the blade rebound
From their bodies,
Still he continued to jump and fight

And stay out of their deadly grasps.

Then as luck and timing would have it
The samurai gave a might swing
Towards the neck of the demon
Who might have been his grandmother
And off came its head.

With a new realization of tactics,
The samurai soon removed the head
Of another demon,
Who might have been his mother,
And finally the last demon,
Who might have been his wife,
Was headless, too.

All three demon bodies sank
To the ground and lay still and dark.

The samurai's energy collapsed
With that final stroke
And he barely managed to
Drag himself back to the hut,
Falling at last onto the mat
Inside.

Late morning sunlight
Filtering through cracks and crevices
In the hut's walls
Awoke the samurai,
He felt better and went outside
Into the clearing
To breath fresh air,
Hear birds sing
And enjoy the warmth of the sun.

Near where the forest began,
He noticed three saplings
Leaning haphazardly towards the ground,
Investigating, he saw that the bark
Of each tree
Had been hacked in several places

And that the green tops of each sapling
Had been separated from their trunks,
The trees were of a kind unknown to him.

He moved back from them, disturbed,
When the saplings began to tilt further
In a slow fall ground-ward,
As if the wood of each tree
Was decaying from within.

Back in the hut,
The samurai made a simple meal
Of dried fish, rice and tea,
He examined his wound,
Which was cooler to the touch – healing.

The remainder of the day
He spent recuperating
And re-sharpening his katana.

After two more days and nights of rest,
The samurai left the hut
To find and rejoin the war
Once more.

The Battle Cry

There once was a tough Samurai
Who had quite the odd loud battle cry,
    "Oooo-la-na-ah-ha-lah-ha-keen"
    Which roughly when translated means,
"I will mince you all up for stir fry!"

Stop! What Goes There?

Hikers in the woods
Often tell a story
Of dangers in the forest
That give them not much glory.

Take the hikers who discover
Deep scratches in the trunks of trees
Tufts of dark brown fur on branches
And scat containing berry seeds
And the small bones of rabbits --
There is a bear in the woods!
Beware!

And when this group of hikers – weary walkers
Near the final mile of a long week's trail
Glance ahead and see a dark form standing there,
And this is when their tired eyes fail,
A hundred yards away "It's the bear"
Someone shouts and bodies momentarily freeze
Before preparing a rapid flee...

But laughter falls instead
The hulking creature has looked back and mooed,
It's a bit of a relieving folly now
As deadly bear turns into harmless cow.

And it becomes a funny story
To be embroidered, shared and teased about
By family and friends
On random weekends...

But let's take a moment and raise our glasses high
For those walking few who don't come back
Who passed hooved tracks and patties flat,
For the hulking form their tricked eyes saw
A few yards up the trail – right there!
Was not the cow *they thought it was*
But turned out to be a bear!

Christmas Poem 2021

Christmas is a time of miracles
And a time of icicles

It is the time for Santa Claus
And magic from the Land of Oz

It is a time of gifts and dreams
Of happy carols and silly memes

It's a time of decorated cookies and fruitcake
And other good eats of the season to partake

It is a time of charity and goodwill to all
Of orchestral music and fancy balls

And truest of all, Christmas is a time of loving you
And you and you and you and you
And you and you and you and you
And you and you and you and you
And you and you and you and you
And you and you and you and you...

The Tolerant Cat and The Little Girl

The sun through the window is just right
As it touches the floor where I have just laid down.
This will not last long, but I have the timing down –
As any cat can do for perfect comfort.
When my ears perk up with the patter of little feet.

I could run and hide, but I just can't resist her.
She is like the favorite of a litter who,
No matter how demanding or annoying
You give into most often and hold onto the longest.
She picks me up and I go limp.

It used to be she tried to carry me by a leg
Or she thought my tail was a handle.
And I had to be gently stern, with a 'Meorr"
And a bat with a clawless paw, –
The young do need some discipline in their training.

She carries me to where she thinks I should be
Which is her play area with the newly understood blocks.
At first she surrounds me in wood while I relax
Then she stacks three blocks each over the next
And on top of them, the ball.

I cannot help myself, I have to strike
The ball rolls swiftly away and I give chase while
The three blocks come tumbling down
And she is laughing as she comes
To where I have corralled the ball and takes it from me.

And so the time passes
And even though I know what will happen again and again
The excitement of the ball appearing on the blocks
To be hit and captured with my paws and taken away
Never leaves me.

But she tires and her queen comes and lifts her to nap time
Which is fine, quite fine, I am ready for my nap time, too.
And although the sun has moved, I know where it will be,
I shall stalk the spot and sleep, instead I sigh,
For dog appears with a wagging tail and a playful eye.

Sunset as Seen by a Young Child of a Physicist

Ker-splash! Hisssssssss!
The sun hits and sizzles down
Into the distant ocean water,
Only to be relit
By the Friends of Fusion
In the morning.

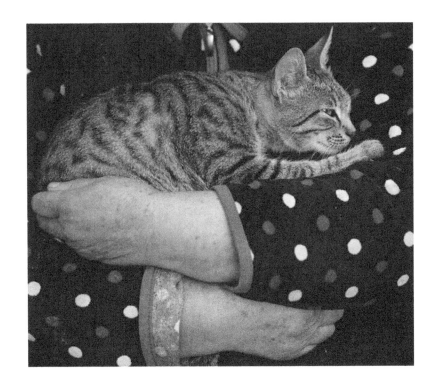

Cat Love

Jump into my lap
And fill me with that warmth
Radiating from your golden heart,
Your needle claws can knead my thighs
Before you settle in,
And begin the purr
That leads to sleep,
And I promise not to move
Until I really have to.

A Child of Many Worlds Photographed Long Ago

"Są'ąh naagháí dóó ił ééhózin ach'é'é."

She is a Navajo
She is an American
She is like any other child
In the world
Alive this day, this year
She is herself.

Her face brightens with smiles
Her eyes pool with tears
She grows up strong
Or struggles with her health,
However it goes
She is herself.

The child takes up the mantle of adulthood
Works to survive
Works to create

She loves
She has children
Or does not –
Traveling the paths
The many worlds
Force her to go,
Still she is herself.

The many years pass
The world sees her now
As an old woman
Or a fierce warrior
Or just another consumer –
One of the billions,
None of that matters,

Inside are her dreams
Inside are her accomplishments
Inside is her experience
Inside is her wisdom,

She is as she as always been
Even as on that day as a child long ago
The bearded man
Took her photograph
For history –
She is herself.

"Ak'ijidí nilį."

Fish Zen

They are mine
But beyond my reach.

The pond floats on the table
But my paw cannot reach inside
A barrier keeps me from my fish.

I am not allowed on the table,
But
The gurgling from the water
Calls me to investigate –
There is a cover on the pond.

I sit on a chair to watch my fish
Swim back and forth,
A hunger grows for them
And then disappears.

I see now only their movements
Here and there, up and down
Hidden, then visible, energy for hours.

No matter what I have tried,
To reach, capture, play and eat them,
I cannot touch.

They are mine
But beyond my reach.

The Australian Child's Assignment to Write a Poem About a Rare Animal

Let me tell you about cuscus, the animal, not the food
Although a meal of couscous, may be stored in a pouch,
And the cuscus, being marsupial, keeps its young in a pouch,
And so there is a similarity there, isn't there?

The 13 kinds of wild cuscus in Australia and New Guinea are nocturnal
The many styles of tamed couscous, steamed wheat – sorghum – bulgar
And other cereals are often served at night
Is that a coincidence?

And now the arguments begin...

Cuscus are arboreal which means they live in trees
But couscous is made from the grains of grasses
And grasses and trees have been fighting for dominance
Over the lands of the earth for 66 million years.

Cuscus eat leaves, fruits, flowers
Small birds, reptiles and eggs,

But they don't eat couscous
People eat couscous, but not cuscus.

People have opposable thumbs and can hold things
Like plates of couscous which they cook,
Cuscus have opposable thumbs and hold onto tree limbs,
But have never held a plate or learned to cook.

Cuscus have prehensile tails like monkeys,
Couscous can contain vegetables and meats like stews,
If you were desperate enough to eat and grill a cuscus
You could place the cooked cuscus into couscous
For dinner.

We sometimes have couscous for dinner with lamb and carrots
But I would rather have a cuscus for a pet,
Although I've heard they bite,
But my parents won't even let me have a cat!

Competing with a Bear

A man and a bear were out fishing,
With growls and insults they were "dishing"
   Each other about
   Who could catch the most trout,
Funny thing is, the man is now missing.

To Parodize

Original:
Oh give me a home where the buffalo roam,
Where the deer and the antelope play,
Where seldom is heard a discouraging word,
And the skies are not cloudy all day.

Parody:
Oh, give me a shake, where its taste is not fake
With chocolate that is organic and fair trade
And the hamburger platter, won't make me grow fatter
Cause it's made from plants grown in the shade.

White Snow Like Fur Covers a Tree in Yosemite

A tree stands with branches wrapped
In the frozen waters of winter
Like an opaque ice sculpture
Or a frosted glass object
Set on on a shelf layered thickly
With sparkling, crystalline snow.

The tree is
Alive, but dormant,
Asleep, but dreaming,
Of new growth in the spring –
Green shoots and white blossoms,
Of birds and summer breezes –
When the Winds of the World
Will move its leaves
And bring news and connection
With all the other trees
That grow on the Earth.

Cat Christmas

They brought the forest
Inside the walls for me,
Surprise!

Then they shouted when
I climbed the tree,
Surprise!

They placed a hundred
Shiny balls up for me,
Surprise!

Then shouted when I
Broke the lowest one,
Surprise!

They placed upon the table
A giant meal for me,
Surprise!

Then shoutest loudest when
I tried to take my share,
Surprise!

They gathered all to sing
Great songs for me,
Surprise!

Next morn they gifted me
A catnip mouse and ball of yarn,
Surprise!

Meowy Christmas!

Bats in a Tourist Cave

Tadarida brasiliensis,
One of 17 species who use Carlsbad Caverns – speaks for them all...

Long have we dwelled in this dark hollow
Ours forever we might say, though,
Time is not something bats follow.

Then the tourists came
To steal our day
How could we sleep
With the voices, the lights, the stumbling of feet
Echoing away?

So we mocked war thundering our wings
Over your heads,
But our crisscrossing flights only seemed
To encourage you more –
The sudden frights, brought you delight
Instead of dread.

Bats are not crazy,
We have learned to accommodate

And sleep only in sectors you do not go,
Still we play our parts –
A selected hundred or so along with their mates
Flash through the airspace above your tallest
Bringing aloud the shrieks of your young
Sounding so much like the squeaks
Our own children have sung.

Lately our numbers have dwindled
Your trespassing presence being more intense
You have brought the white nose disease
For which we have little defense,
Worse yet, we grow hungrier, too,
Both leading to why
We are becoming so few
Now hundreds of thousands instead of the millions
Less every birth cycle,
Where is our food?

When the sun turns red, then violet
A glorious throng into the skies we kite
But where are the moths, crickets,
Mosquitos and gnats,
Vanished it seems
Are the insects of the night –
What have you done out there?

Bring It All Home

Back to the woods go walking
Out in nature on a sunny day,
You may work up an appetite
For some sweet treat,
An apple or an orange sounds fine,
But once you've finished off the fruit
Don't throw what's left
Into the brush –
An apple core or those orange rinds
Is not good food for forest folks
Please bag up all your leftovers
When you're done
And bring them home -
Leave no trace behind.

Sometimes on a hike
A candy bar
Is just the thing to eat,
But animals have sensitive noses
And the wrappers those treats
Come covered in,
Smell like sweet food to skunks
And deer and bears and
Others in the forest.

Would you eat the wrapping
From a Snickers Bar?
No!
Nor should woodland creatures
Be tempted to
Because someone threw
Without a care
Such packaging away,
It's some strange food to eat
Think shy squirrels
And all the rest who caper in the wild –
Please be kind,

Take home those scraps of trash
When you retire from the fields,
And leave no trace behind.

Be mindful of all
The animals in Nature,
The food your bring is not for them
It's for you, your friends and family –
Watch out!
Bears can develop a taste for trial mix
When thoughtlessly dropped within the parks,
Don't be surprised if they come hunting for more
And you are the substitute snack,
Do you hear the bear's roar?

Way too many deer die
From stomachs stuffed with plastic bags
That blow off the trail into the bramble
And are nibbled on,

Squirrels forget to teach their young
The ways to hunt for nuts,
If there is tossed out, ready-made
Human grub
That is easier to find and eat then
Their natural food hard foraged for
In the patches where they run.

The beautiful lands of forests and fields
Are those wild creatures' homes –
Don't be a messy guest!
I think you'll find
A special peace of mind
When you are kind,
And leave no trace behind.

My Mind has Drawn a Blank!

I've been in a fog all morning
And my lecture's almost due
The classroom bell will soon ring out
What subject was I going to do?

Right! The topic is a reptile
What was its family name?
With over 1500 species members
Scincidae hits me like a flame!

Green ones, blue-tongued, red-faced
Damn, I'm feeling very vexed –
I can't recall their common name
In truth my mind's a wreck...

Last night I had too much to drink
If only I could, come on think!
Oh, my blasted brain is on the blink,
They're not just lizards, they are _____!

The Snake River

I once snagged a fish
On the Snake River
My hook fastening on its side
As it swam by –
This is not an honorable way
To catch a trout
Though its flesh was crispy sweet
When grilled in a campfire pan
That night.

The Snake River is a windy one,
Looking from above
Like a giant rattler swishing
Side to side
Through rugged terrain,
And the Snake's water at dawn
Is so cold sometimes
It feels like fangs are biting

Your ankles,
But the real question to ask
Is: Are the fish biting?

There is a spot along the Snake
Where the pines come close
To either bank,
But leave enough breathing space
For easy walking
And with room to cast your rod –
And the only things that exist
Are you, the river and the trees
And the distant Teton Mountains
Which look like shards of purple, blue glass
Stabbing the sky,
Still drizzled
With the thick white frosting
Of winter snow –
Which reminds me
Of the fresh baked cinnamon rolls
And their sugary icing
I had with my coffee at a café
Two days ago.

Standing here with my line
In the rushing, rustling waters of the Snake
A slight breeze pushing a piney scent
From the trees,
The sun warm, but not yet hot
Looking at the Tetons,
So small in the distance,
But so magnificent in reality,
There is no better place
To be.

The Cat and the Day of the Special Fog

In years past, there is a time
When the sun disappears sooner
And rises later,
When the winds change, too,
Blowing stronger, yet still warm, East and South.
And with the winds go,
In groups of 3 or 5,
Flying things,
Enough to get my attention –
Too few to act.

This year, this day,
As the door opened out to the porch
There was a vibration in the air,
Not the buzz of bees, but...
The sky was brown and grey
And moving!
There was a fog of dragonflies
Thousands and thousands, no millions of tiny bodies,
Fleeing from the nearby river
Going somewhere else –
Too many not to act.

I leapt to strike seven
In one blow,
Then sprang again to hit eight,
And down the street other cats
Were jumping, filling the air like trout –
Attacking the sky.

Every cat throughout the town
Was jumping,
And above, the birds were diving down,
Then up and around
Filling their up their beaks
With crunches.

All day the fog of dragonflies
Rolled on,
Until the winds died away
And bone weary, I crept back inside,
With thousands to my credit,
And went to my nest to sleep,
The sleep of a MOST glorious day!

Friends

Like a special star
First to twinkle every night
My friendship with you

The Girl

Child of golden light
On her own journey through time
Her story to write

A Dog's Dog

Give me a mutt
A regular mutt
And I'll show you the best of the breed.

You can keep your Labradoodles
And your teacup Pekingese
Your Chihuahuas in tight sweaters
And those little fluffs that blow away
If you sneeze –
I guess they're nice to look at
Or have sit upon your lap,
But there not real dogs to me.

Get me a dog that
Runs through the hills
And returns with a grin when called,
Can catch a mouse, swim a river,
Fetch a stick, raise a paw,
Barks out danger, but stays when it is told,
And whose tail is always wagging fast,
When you come home.

Is there for you in hard times –
Whines softly when you're blue,
Mourns a death with lonesome howls,
Lays a muzzle in your lap
When sympathy and comfort
Is your need.

Whose warm body thaws cold hands,
Makes you laugh with funny dances,
And watches o'er your children
With the fiercest loyalty.

Three words of advice are enough
Get a mutt!

A Little Doggerel

It has come to me,
Though it may seem odd,
That Bagel, my favorite dog,
From her actions I have formed
A resolution most lucid,
To acknowledge her as
A bona fido, canine fluid druid.

For once a month
The bitch insists we go,
To the woods, and lo,
She seeks out special sacred trees,
And sniffs the roots and trunks,
All roundabout,
Then lifts her leg in prayer and pees.

The Pane of Perception

Through a kitchen window
Witness the new neighbor
Over ensuing weeks
Trim trees and bushes of their foliage
Dig up old flower beds
And place bulbs and seedlings about
Along with two statues of the Buddha
Decorating either side of the front yard.

One sunny morning between the waves
Of rain that scour the coastline,
This time of year,
See a crow land on the rooftop
Across the street stand still
And stare at the Buddha nearest it.

The minutes flow, the bird is transfixed
In silent contemplation, then
In a flurry, flits further along the roof
To stop and gaze at the second Buddha statue
With rapt attention, before
Flying away.

Was the bird recalling a past life,
Was it building up momentum
Towards a future one,
Or just experiencing a span of
"Being Here Now"
Like Huxley's Island Myna?

A skeptic would whisper
It was merely looking with intensity
For insects to devour
Lured out from the wet ground
By the unexpected rays of the sun.

Then why did,
On the next light filled morning –

Warm enough to push up the window
To call in the breeze,
The crow return to the roof
With a bell on a string entangled
Around one leg and claws.

The crow does a hopping dance
On the tiled roof,
The bell tinkles faintly, rhythmically –
A little Buddha Bop
Before dislodging, string and all, to
Bounce, bounce, bounce up against
The Buddha statue's back,
"Caw, caw," the crow cries
Before it flies
Off into
The radiant skies.

Everywhere about
Outside my window,
Are bits of awareness,
Encased in bodies,
Wandering this crazy world.

The Patient Frog

A frog is sitting quiet and still
Near a pond.

When a fly lands in the middle of its back,
The frog stays sitting quiet and still.

When the fly starts walking forward
The frog remains sitting
Quiet and still
Even though it feels
Each sticky fly foot going
Squish-plop
Across its green skin.

Step by step crawls the fly
Pausing a moment
Between the frog's eyes,

The frog sits quiet and still.

Then onward creeps the fly
Reaching the frog's
Spread apart nose,

The frog sits quiet and still.

The fly steps onto the frog's lips,

Snap!

The frog's mouth opens and shut so quick
It crushes the fly before it could flit
Then, with a "whooping" sound
The frog sucks in the fly
From between its lips
And swallows it.

The frog, without having to
Lash out its long tongue,
Has caught a nice, juicy morsel
Of savory bug lunch.

The frog sits quiet and still.

Choose Love

What I love about love
Is companionship
Of wanting to share with someone.

Of warmth
Which sometimes turns to
Passion
To excitement and the feeling
That anything is possible
And our smiles are their widest.

Everyone and everything is wonderful –
Fear has disappeared.

It is a bright sunny morning of freedom
Where everyday is a day off
And the world is the way
It's supposed to be.

Cheshire Pizza: Your Order is Ready

Diverse cats want different foods
Topped on their pizza dish
Except every pie should include
Fresh blue tuna fish.

Tabbies then add on liver
Siamese request rats
Squid makes Manxes quiver
Calicos demand bats.

Shorthairs prefer voles
Black cats chicken gizzards
Persians choose moles
Longhairs sliced lizard.

Use gopher Sphynxes scream
Inside the pie crust
And a free bowl of cream
Is our specialty touch.

Future Children's School Poem

How do we build our houses?
With strong boards formed from hemp
And pressed bricks of mycelium.

How do we power our homes?
By harvesting the sun
And utilizing the powers
Of chemistry and physics.

How do we keep our lands clean?
By reusing and recycling and regulation
And by asking our friends –
The bacteria, algae and fungi to help.

How do we make ourselves strong?
By playing outside and walking the land
Be developing skills and absorbing knowledge
And learning to think for ourselves.

How do we have food and know joy?
By respecting all life around us
And knowing each species has its purpose
And its gift – including ourselves.

Neurons Regenerated

A scientific miracle of rare device
A protein gel to cure
Spinal paralysis in mice.

Now Little Timmy Mouse
Can throw away his crutches
And others leave their chairs with wheels
To walk or scurry once again
Through our pantries and wheat fields.

Soon men and women, too, will find
Their ills profoundly cured
Their nervous system cells rebuilt, re-twined
So once again they'll walk, and dance and move secure.

So thank you scientific teams
For all the tedious, yet valuable, research you do
Which shows this dark world is a far better place
Than it may seem
'Cause you scientists keep amazing us
With your breakthroughs after breakthroughs!

Hope

Children should never have to carry
The weight of the world.
And yet and yet —
We keep failing them.
And yet and yet —
They keep surprising us
By growing up
And doing better than we did.

Haven't you noticed?

Sometimes I lose money –
Dollars on the street,
A twenty left behind,
And cash I don't know where it went,
But it was in my pocket
A little while ago,

And after cursing myself
For my idiocy
I let it go
By making a little wish:
Whosever hands my loss falls into,
They be ones that need it more than I
That day.

I have no clue if the world
Works that way,
Perhaps one day we will build
A colossal AI of such enormity
That it can tag each puff of wind,
Or watch the fall of every sparrow
And know the results that come
From everything –
My God, what a being that would be,

But I will just go on trusting
That more good, times a million,
Comes about
Than all the bad news chronicled
In every media's headline every day.

Generosities and kindness,
Even the unconscious ones,
Happen all around us,
Haven't you noticed?

The Dolphin Caught

Haul the nets, crew, haul the nets!

Damn that bottlenose,
Why have sonar
If you don't use it?
Why let intelligence fail,
By distraction,
And get tangled
In our nets, head to tail
For some lousy mackerel?

Separate her out, crew, separate her out
We'll trade her with a ship
Going East
Where they still eat dolphin meat –
Chopped and grilled or stewed,
Pounds and pounds of protein
In that mammal, crew.

It is a sad thing,
When the smartest dolphin
Of the sea loses out
On 20 more years of swimming life
Dying in a fishing catch,
But we have our own people to feed
And profits to get,
So lower the nets, crew, drop the nets
Back into the deep, blue sea.

The Dragonfly by Lothar Meggendorfe

The Same, Yet Different

One day,
A catfish and a dragonfly
Had a conversation
About when they were young.

"It is my understanding,"
Said the catfish,
"That when I was my youngest,
"I was an egg!"

"Why, me, too,"
Replied the dragonfly, tilting his head,
"Who knew,
"We had so much in common?"

"Then," the catfish said dramatically,
"I became a fingerling,
"Swimming in the river
"Eating the tiniest insects."

"My, my," said the dragonfly,
"I became a nymph, and I too,
"Swam in the river
"Seeking tiny bits of life to eat."

"I grew bigger and swam further."

"I grew wings and leapt into the sky."

"I can leap into the sky," said the fish,
"For a moment, anyway,
"But must always return
"To the river."

"Oh, I can never swim in water again,
"The air is my world,
"And plants to rest on."

"It is only the river, for me,
"But maybe, one day, I'll go to the sea,
"Which is water, too."

Both went quiet,
Then the fish exclaimed,
"Funny how we started the same way,
"And grew to be so different."

"Hmmm, yes," said the dragonfly,
A bit distractedly,
For he had just noticed
 A swarm of mosquitoes coming near,
"It was nice talking with you."
And he flew off.

"Bye" said the catfish, faintly,
A bit distracted herself,
For she had noticed a school
Of small fry clouding the water
Below her,
She was ready for a snack
And dived.

A Bird Poem

Plenty of birds dive or swim
Eagles in the air, ducks in water

Numbers of flightless birds are fewer –
Grebes and rails and teal species,
Unexpectedly, with ostriches and emus are
Included, but none are as cute as

Nature's grounded, waddling divers and
Swimmers – the penguins!

All the Forests Everywhere

How funny it is
In a small café
On a side street in Portland
You should notice her
And she should notice you
And you suddenly see

All the forests everywhere
And all the homes that dwell within
And all the world
And all beyond
In her amber eyes

And your smiles say
That love is where
It's always been
Waiting here
For you

Stay Away from that Crazy Man!

Oh, he's just trying to scare us
The crazy old man named Maris,
But that elongating tooth!
He's turned into a wolf!
Ruuuun! He is going to tear us.

The Gaze

There once was a person so rich
His/Her homes held mounds of diamonds
And mountains of gold
And were surrounded by the choicest sections
Of land.

One day she/he ventured out into the streets
Of a city, to stretch the legs
And enjoy the morning sunshine.

Being the finest of fitness of a specimen
From trainers, nutritionists, dance teachers
And exercise equipment money can provide,
It was ironic that a small protuberance
In the sidewalk should trip him/her up,
But down she/he fell hard.

A stranger knelt down beside him/her
Then helped her/him to stand up.

The stranger was silent
And as he/she looked up
Into the stranger's face, to say "thanks,"
Their gazes met and from the stranger's eyes
Came the strongest force of love
That herself/himself never felt before.

He/She could not find her/his tongue to speak
The stranger gave a pat upon his/her shoulder,
Turned, and vanished into the crowd.

He/She was different after that
For she/he now knew
There was something more important
Than all the material goods
In the world!

The Buzz of the Day

Bees fascinate children
And are scary, too,
Remember running from a bee,
Yet still in love with the buzzing
sound?

The first bee sting is an initiation
Not into a new stage of fear,
But to a new understanding of carefulness
As you might learn
When a dog nips you in play –

A recognition to let bees do their job
Of flying into flowers undisturbed
And they will leave you alone
To play and run or pick an apple from a tree.

Bees are the guardians of the harvest,
Without their constant work,
So many flowers and fruits and vegetables
Would disappear from our world.

In the summer sun,
It is the buzz that grows in harmony
As bee after bee join in,
Gathering pollen and pollinating
The garden,
That calls to me,
An almost sacred sound that reassures
That the world is the way it should be...
And soon there will be honey!

Poor Little Messy Jessy

There was a young child name of Jessica
Who had a problem of making a mess-i-ca
     Her parents were wrought
     And too often fought
And the child's behavior went unaddressed-i-ca.

Wish Upon a Star

There is a star
For every wish
You wish to make

Let your imagination soar
To its far space
And orbit that distant sun

Gather its light
With your hands and mind
And weave a dream

Return to Earth
And share its glow
With everyone around you

The dream may turn real
Then go on on its own
And you grow, too

Wishes and dreams and reality
Become what they become
But maybe its true

That when you wish sincerely
Upon a star
At night

You can touch
A little bit
Of everything to come

I Am Here

I am here;
I've read all the poems
In the book –
Learned this and that,
But mostly I just want
To say
I am here,
It's important sometimes
To remember that.

Image Credits

About the Author

The author currently resides in a small coastal town in Southern Oregon where he owns a small photography publishing business. He lives a simple life with his wife of longstanding, writing poetry and stories and non-fiction books.

More Books by the Author

 "Frankenstein's Monster in Oz" – This book tells the story of how Frankenstein's Monster comes to Oz and what happens to him there. It is available on Amazon at https://www.amazon.com/Frankensteins-Monster-Carl-Scott-Harker/dp/1707291365.

 "Poems By My Cat" – These poems reveal how cats view the world around them. The book can be found on Amazon here: https://www.amazon.com/Poems-Cat-Carl-Scott-Harker/dp/1793903239.

 "The Mad Artist: A Sherlock Holmes Story in Free Verse" – This book presents a new Sherlock Holmes story and is written in free verse and features the artist Vincent Van Gogh. It is available on Amazon at https://amzn.to/36nWvf0.

 "Vampire Limericks and Other Bits of Humor" – This book collects my early work prior to the year 2000 (mostly) and includes limericks, cartoons and a short story. Here is the link to the book on Amazon: https://amzn.to/2IsPUbg.

 "50 Great Poems to Read & Perform Out Loud" – This is a collection of the best poems ever written. The book can be found here: https://amzn.to/2zz8GFT.

 "Seeds of Poetry: 21 Methods to Inspire Your Poetry and Other Creative Writings" – a book featuring writing tips with examples to inspire the writing of your own poetry and other creative works. You will find this book here: https://amzn.to/2HtMpO7.

 "100 Classic Poems to Read at Christmas Time" – Here is a collection of some of the best Christmas poems written. The book can be found here: https://www.amazon.com/dp/B07J9YS7QK

 "Samurai Weapons" – This book looks at the weapons and the culture of the classic Japanese Samurai through essays, illustrations and poetry. The book is available on Amazon at https://amzn.to/45h8NT7.

"Classic Art of Absinthe" – This book collects the best of the classic artwork about absinthe from the makers of absinthe, those who wanted absinthe banned and the artists of the time (mid-1800's to early 1900's). It is available on Amazon at https://www.amazon.com/Classic-Absinthe-Carl-Scott-Harker/dp/1653501189.

 "Trees and Flowers of Vincent Van Gogh" – This book collects the best examples of trees and flowers painted by the artist /Vincent Van Gogh. Here is the link for this pictorial book: https://amzn.to/3p3aaII.

 "Exploring The Universe: The Art of Space" – Through the use of instruments such as the Hubble Space Telescope, scientists have captured the colorful art that space itself creates. Here is the link: https://www.amazon.com/Exploring-Universe-Carl-Scott-Harker-ebook/dp/B077XQRPQL

 "The Van Gogh Poems and Other Poetry" – This book features a collection of poems written in late 2019 and early 2020. The first seventeen poems in this work were inspired by paintings of Vincent Van Gogh. The book is available on Amazon at https://amzn.to/38Hq6Tg.

 "Above Us Only Sky" – This book of poetry features poems written between late April, 2020 to late October, 2020. You will find this book here: https://amzn.to/38kb83R.

 "Words of Change" – This book of poetry features poems written from late October of 2020 through May, 2021. You will find this book here: https://amzn.to/3Kxzjy2.

 **"Lyrics Looking for a Musician"** – Discover poetry of the outside life in the physical world – social poems, poems about other people and personal experiences. And explore poems of the inner life – poems of the mind and science and poems of the spiritual path. This book can be found on Amazon here: https://amzn.to/3t1icNI.

 "Am I Indigenous and Other Poems" – A collection of poems written between late 2016 and Autumn 2019. This book can be found on Amazon here: https://www.amazon.com/Am-I-Indigenous-Other-Poems/dp/1689862424.

 "An Engineer of Words" – This twelfth book collects a selection of poems written between January 1, 2022 and August 31, 2022. There are story poems, biographical poems, silly poems, poems that rhyme and many that do not. You will find this book here: https://amzn.to/3DFchDI.

Made in the USA
Las Vegas, NV
17 December 2023

82357078R00044